Bomji and Spotty's Frightening Adventure

Anne Westcott and C. C. Alicia Hu

Illustrated by Ching-Pang Kuo

Jessica Kingsley Publishers
London and Philadelphia

First published in 2018
by Jessica Kingsley Publishers
73 Collier Street
London N1 9BE, UK
and
400 Market Street, Suite 400
Philadelphia, PA 19106, USA

www.jkp.com

Library of Congress Cataloging in Publication Data
A CIP catalog record for this book is available from the
Library of Congress

British Library Cataloguing in Publication Data
A CIP catalogue record for this book is available from
the British Library

ISBN 978 1 78592 770 6
eISBN 978 1 78450 670 4

Printed and bound in the UK

books in the same series

How Little Coyote Found His Secret Strength
A Story About How to Get Through Hard Times
ISBN 978 1 78592 771 3
eISBN 978 1 78450 671 1

How Sprinkle the Pig Escaped the River of Tears
A Story About Being Apart From Loved Ones
ISBN 978 1 78592 769 0
eISBN 978 1 78450 669 8

Introduction

The body possesses innate capacities to ensure we make it through distressing situations. This inborn wisdom of the body inspired me to develop Sensorimotor Psychotherapy[SM] (SP) decades ago. I have made it my life's work to elucidate this largely untapped resource so that we can engage it to help ourselves and others heal from severe stress, trauma, and attachment disruption.

The Hidden Strengths Therapeutic Children's Books series captures this essential spirit and intention of Sensorimotor Psychotherapy[SM]. The authors render the core concepts of this approach accessible to both caregivers and young people struggling in the aftermath of overwhelming experiences. The stories do so with sensitivity and particular attention to illustrating the bodily experience of the child in an engaging and compelling manner.

Understanding the language of the body helps us make sense of the often confusing behaviors following trauma and separation from loved ones. We freeze, run away, collapse, fight, hide, cry for someone bigger and wiser to help us, and even dissociate or do things we wouldn't normally do, like steal, to make it through. These instinctive bodily survival defenses are automatically engaged in times of threat. Each of us employs the defensive response(s) that will work best in a particular moment given the immediate circumstances, so there is no single best survival strategy. These compelling stories emphasize the hidden strengths in the characters' survival behaviors, staying true to the foundational principle of SP that the physical actions taken are the person's best attempt to respond to the situation they face.

Over time, we develop habits of defensive responses, often repeatedly engaging just one or two survival defenses. These then become our default behaviors in the face of subsequent threats, which is compassionately and wisely illustrated by the appealing characters in the stories in the series. Anyone helping children will find new ways to look at the often challenging and misunderstood behaviors children display after stress. The stories also encourage caregivers and children to become curious about the survival functions these behaviors may serve.

As the authors, both trained in Sensorimotor Psychotherapy[SM], describe how the characters adapt to challenging circumstances, the body's wisdom is revealed. Each character favors a different survival defense, which is cleverly portrayed through the character's movement, posture, and physiology. The pictures and rich descriptive text convey the real-life bodily and emotional experience of so many children, without evaluation, judgement, or interpretation. The stories describe events and behaviors from each character's viewpoint, offering a variety of perspectives. Doing so enhances understanding of how the body responds and influences the meaning we make of what we see, hear, and feel. The ability to gain perspective, to stay curious, and to experiment are core to Sensorimotor Psychotherapy[SM] and woven into each story. Children will feel relieved and understood as they recognize themselves and their peers in the myriad struggles of the characters. Behaviors children might have perceived as ineffective or worse, a confirmation of their own badness, may very well be transformed into a strength that can be adapted to help them thrive. Our bodies adapt via movement, posture, and physiology.

The supplements following the stories will help caregivers recognize the signs of these survival strengths in the simple body clues of gesture, posture, tone of voice, facial expression, eye gaze, and movement. This is what I have termed the "somatic narrative" core to Sensorimotor Psychotherapy[SM]. When one understands the language the body uses to tell the story of distress, puzzling and confusing behaviors by children begin to make more sense. When we can make sense of our children's behaviors, we are better equipped to respond in flexible and sensitive ways to help our children feel better in their bodies, hearts, and minds.

Pat Ogden, Founder, Sensorimotor Psychotherapy Institute, 2017

About the Hidden Strengths Series

This book is part of a series for children who have lived through extremely stressful times. The series is inspired by Sensorimotor Psychotherapy℠, a unique approach to trauma treatment developed by Dr. Pat Ogden. The series is designed to present children's distress in a realistic yet digestible way.

The authors have carefully crafted the stories so as to reduce sensory stimulus and not overwhelm traumatized children. You will notice this in the language chosen: simple yet descriptive, in a way that seeks to highlight hidden strengths in potentially shaming moments. You will also see this in the images as they shift away from bright color to grays at particularly tense moments. The very crafting of the book was guided by the principles and knowledge of Sensorimotor Psychotherapy℠ and the authors' deep understanding of children. This attention to the reader's experience makes the book useful to anyone caring for traumatized children.

We possess many kinds of strengths to get through challenging times. Some are obvious and some are harder to see. Many of these hidden strengths live in our bodies and leap to our rescue instantly, bypassing our thinking. These strengths try to keep us safe in times of danger when we have to act fast and may not have help around.

These books will help you and your child gain understanding and appreciation for the amazing abilities that live inside of you. By sharing these stories with your child, these books will help them to reduce feelings of shame, recognize that problematic feelings and behaviors can be a response to stressful times, and feel better in their body.

OTHER BOOKS IN THE SERIES

You and your child will meet several characters over and over again when you explore the series. The animals' lives intertwine in unexpected ways. Gaining a deeper window into each character changes our feelings toward the animals. The series is crafted to generate curiosity, empathy, and perspective-taking in the reader. These capacities are stunted by trauma and chronic stress.

READING TIPS

Find a space where you are both in a relaxed and playful mood. Allow 20–30 minutes to explore and talk about the content.

1. Allow children to decide the reading speed. Some children enjoy exploring the details in pictures more than the storyline. Some children may have emotional reactions to the content and want to skip or fast-forward to a later part of the story.

2. Children are very creative. Your child may ask questions you can't answer. Support your child's curiosity by encouraging them to come up with their own answers.

3. Suggested activities are provided at the end of each book. They are designed to help deepen the learning from the story through all your child's senses.

Bomji the Rabbit and Spotty the Cat are not just friends.

They are the BEST of friends!

Bomji and Spotty go to school together. After school, Bomji and Spotty play together.

Bomji and Spotty are different.

Bomji is a boy. Spotty is a girl.

Bomji lives with his mom. Spotty lives with her grandma.

Bomji is brainy. Spotty is sporty.

But they enjoy each other's company.

One sunny day after school Bomji asked Spotty, "Do you want to come to the meadow with me and pick some flowers? I want to take a big bunch home for my mom."

"That's a great idea!" said Spotty. "My grandma would love to have some flowers on the dining table tonight."

Bomji and Spotty ran to the meadow at the edge of the forest. There, they found many sweet-smelling flowers. Red, yellow, orange, pink, and purple!

As they were plucking flowers, they got an odd feeling inside. Something was out of place.

Then, they heard a tree branch break in the forest. They turned toward the sound and saw a big shadow moving in the trees.

Their hearts quickened and they darted behind a raspberry bush.

Bomji and Spotty peered through the brambles. Something big and dark was coming.

Oh no! It was a coyote!

Bomji froze. His body started to tremble.

Spotty grew taller. Her body was charged with strength.

Spotty watched the coyote get closer and closer. She was ready to run away, but she felt Bomji's body against her arm, solid like a stone, still like a statue.

Bomji could not run, and the coyote got even closer...

Before Spotty could even think, she jumped out of the bushes. She yelled at the coyote, "Hey, I'll bet you can't run as fast as I can!"

The coyote stopped short. Spotty looked up to see big sharp pointy teeth.

Without another word, Spotty turned and ran into the forest and felt a hidden strength rising in her body. Her legs pumped with energy; her lungs burned like fire. The coyote chased Spotty. Spotty ran faster and faster. The coyote chased faster and faster! Somehow, Spotty's body kept her going, always one step ahead.

Spotty's legs tired; the coyote was getting too close. She spotted a tall tree and leapt up the trunk just in time. To escape the coyote's big teeth, she scrambled higher and higher to an upper branch. From there, Spotty looked down on the coyote. She saw him trying and trying to get up the trunk; each time he fell back down.

Spotty knew she was safe in the tree because coyotes cannot climb.

Smugly, Spotty watched the coyote give up and walk back to the dark forest.

As she watched the coyote slip out of sight, Spotty began to breathe deeper and her body relaxed.

She felt the sun warming her back and the breeze caressing her face. Her body felt a deep sense of calm.

From her high perch, Spotty looked all around. She could just see the meadow in the distance. She thought, "I live in a beautiful place!"

Her limbs softened. Her eyelids became droopy. She began to doze.

"Wait a minute! Where is Bomji?"

Spotty sprang up!

Spotty remembered her frightened friend and dashed back to find him.

As Spotty neared the bush, she could see Bomji crouching behind it, super still. Bomji's eyes were wide and his shoulders were frozen stiff. Bomji's body held a hidden strength: stillness. By staying motionless, the coyote had passed right by him when chasing Spotty.

Spotty rushed over to Bomji, held his hand, and whispered, "Don't worry, Bomji, the coyote has gone!" Hearing the danger had passed, Bomji felt a sense of relief, and his body started quivering. The shaking helped feeling come back to Bomji's frozen body. Bomji found his voice; he mumbled, "My legs are wobbly and I cannot walk!"

Spotty didn't know what to do. She carefully pulled Bomji out of the bush and carried him all the way back home.

The road home was so long and so quiet.

Spotty was afraid she would say the wrong thing and upset Bomji. Bomji was embarrassed and confused about why his legs felt wobbly.

So much had happened. It seemed so long ago that they had started picking flowers.

Day after day, Bomji and Spotty did not talk about what had happened.

Night after night, Bomji dreamed of running away from a whole pack of coyotes.

Even though the coyote had gone away, Bomji didn't feel safe anymore.

Things that used to make him happy didn't cheer him up like before.

Sometimes, he felt outside his body.

Sometimes, things looked blurry and far, far away.

Sometimes, he pictured the coyote's big teeth.

Bomji didn't want to tell anybody he was scared.

Bomji heard a little voice inside his body, whispering, "Be quiet, stay still."

He kept his feelings hidden inside his body, but he had so many of them that it became harder and harder for him to stop them from bursting out.

Spotty kept a close eye on her friend Bomji.

At lunch, Spotty saw Sprinkle the Pig bump into Bomji. Bomji snapped and started yelling, so angry he did not even know what he was saying. "Hey! Watch where you're going, you stupid pig!"

When Spotty heard Bomji yelling, she was startled and worried. Bomji had always been a kind, thoughtful friend. She had never heard Bomji speak like this before.

Spotty was confused, and her eyes welled up with tears. She needed help to know what to do.

She looked around the schoolyard and spotted Teacher Owl.

Spotty told Teacher Owl everything. How the coyote had chased her and Bomji, how she had distracted the coyote, how Bomji froze, and how he could not walk right on the way home. How, ever since then, Bomji had been acting strange.

Teacher Owl and Spotty went looking for Bomji. They found him alone under a tree. "Bomji, you have a nice shady spot here," said Teacher Owl. "May we join you?"

As Spotty sat down next to his friend, Teacher Owl gently asked, "Bomji, it seems things have been hard for you lately? Spotty told me all about the coyote."

When Bomji heard the word "coyote," he froze again. His body was right back in the meadow, frozen behind the raspberry bush. He began to feel sick to his stomach. It was hard to breathe, and he even felt a bit dizzy.

Teacher Owl saw Bomji's face turn white and his body shrink—Bomji was lost in the memory! Teacher Owl would have to help bring Bomji back.

"Come, walk with us," said Teacher Owl. "Walking can help us feel the strength in our bodies."

Bomji was a little bit wobbly, so Spotty took his paw.

When Bomji felt the warmth of his friend's grasp, it reminded him that he was not alone.

"Look, orange flowers blooming! What colors do each of you like?" asked Teacher Owl.

Teacher Owl knew that Bomji would have to turn his head and look around to answer her question. She hoped this simple movement would be enough to help Bomji leave the bad memory.

Spotty burst out, "We like the bee in the blue sky!"

Bomji slowly looked around at the flowers. "I hadn't even noticed the flowers growing in our school playground—when did these come out?"

Spotty shrugged her shoulders. "Oh, maybe a week ago?"

Bomji shyly giggled.

With a gentle smile, Teacher Owl explained, "Bomji, since you were scared by the coyote, so much was happening inside you. You may have missed many things. Now you and Spotty are back together again!"

Bomji still felt weak, but a warmth spread through his limbs, his body softened, and he felt safe again.

Then, without knowing why, Bomji began to cry. He felt embarrassed.

Teacher Owl whispered, "Tears come when our bodies feel safe again. Bomji, you are safe now. The danger is over."

When Bomji heard this, his cries became bigger and louder. His whole body let out all his fright from the coyote.

Teacher Owl reassured Bomji, "It's okay, let your tears come; they will stop on their own in a few minutes."

The next day, Bomji found Teacher Owl in the schoolyard. They sat down next to each other.

Teacher Owl reminded Bomji that yesterday he had learned how to move away from a bad memory and feel safer.

Now, they were ready to talk about the coyote. Teacher Owl gave Bomji some paper and crayons, and he drew pictures of what he had gone through. He talked and drew. He put all the pieces of his story together.

Later that day, Bomji saw Spotty and asked her to play.

Spotty was relieved. Bomji seemed to be himself again.

"Let's build a spaceship to go on an adventure!" Spotty offered.

Bomji answered, "I know just where to find the wood blocks we need."

Bomji and Spotty are not just friends. They are the BEST of friends!

Let's Talk About Bomji and Spotty's Scary Adventure

Remember how Bomji became frozen when he saw the coyote?

Our bodies know how to become small and still when there is danger. By not moving, Bomji made it harder for the coyote to spot him. Remember how the coyote noticed the sudden movements and noise Spotty made, yet the coyote looked right past Bomji who was still as a statue? Deep inside, Bomji lived this age-old hidden strength: keeping still when facing danger.

If you were Bomji, how would you hide? What would you need to feel better after the danger had passed?

Remember how Spotty's body was full of strength so she could run from the coyote?

Our bodies know how to fill our arms and legs with energy for running from danger—this was Spotty's hidden strength.

When was the last time you were able to run really fast to get away from something? What does it feel like when you are able to get away successfully?

Play Time

LET'S MAKE BELIEVE

Now it is time to make believe we are Bomji and Spotty at different times in the story. Let's "take on" the characters' bodies. Taking on means you each try to copy and mirror the animal's posture and then move while staying in character. This way, we can explore the hidden body strengths Bomji and Spotty have. Parent Tip: If time is short, you can skip some of these, but we recommend you always finish on the last one.

Can you and your parent take on Bomji's and Spotty's bodies when they are picking flowers? (Go to page 7)
Parent Tip: Observe your own body and your child's body. Try describing what you each see in the other and what you feel inside your own body!

...take on Bomji's body when he meets the coyote? (Go to page 9)
Parent Tip: Invite the child to look at their body and your body: arms, legs, torso, neck, head. Describe what the parts feel like or look like. Are they tight like a cord or mushy like mashed potatoes? Do they feel warm or cold?

...take on Spotty's body when she challenges the coyote? (Go to page 10)
Parent Tip: Notice which part of your child's body is full of energy. If you had to read your child's body language, what would it say?

...take on Spotty's body when she runs away from the coyote? (Go to page 11)
Parent Tip: Invite the child to run in SLOW motion and exaggerate the body movement. Observe the strength in the legs.

...take on Spotty's body after she escaped from the coyote and climbed up the tree branch? (Go to page 13)
Parent Tip: How does it feel to succeed in escaping? What in your body tells you that you are safe now? (Check your heartbeat, your muscles, your breathing...)

...take on Bomji's body at school when Sprinkle the Pig bumps him? (Go to page 22)
Parent Tip: What sounds would you make in this posture? How does it feel to use your foot to stomp on the ground to express the anger?

...take on Spotty's and Bomji's bodies when they are looking at flowers with Teacher Owl? (Go to page 29)
Parent Tip: Invite the child to stand where you are. Try to look around without moving your head; pay attention to what you are seeing. Then, let's slowly add some head movement. Notice how far you can turn your head; notice what you can see after adding a wider range of movement!

...take on Bomji's body when Teacher Owl is patiently listening to everything Bomji has to say? (Go to page 31)
Parent Tip: Parent, can you take on Teacher Owl's body? What feelings do each of you have inside your body? When both of you do this, what do you notice right now together? Describe how your muscles feel, your heart, your feelings. When would you need this in your life?

Guide for Grown-Ups

NEW VOCABULARY AND STORY GUIDE

This story briefly introduced survival defenses and the orienting response shared by all humans when encountering danger or overwhelming stress. All these defenses can be helpful in some situations and not helpful in others, and we don't always have a choice about which one our body chooses to use. Please help children to see that both Bomji and Spotty handled the situation as best as they could.

HIDDEN STRENGTH: ACTIVE DEFENSE (FIGHT, FLIGHT)

When there is danger, our bodies automatically want to fight back or run away. If we successfully execute an action to protect or to defend ourselves, we often feel a sense of triumph. Spotty the Cat successfully challenged and ran from the coyote; therefore, she experienced a sense of relaxation afterward.

Bomji, startled by Sprinkle the Pig's bump, fought back by yelling to protect himself. Because Bomji's body was still flooded by the traumatic stress, he raged instead of responding in a more appropriate, firm way.

page 9

page 11

page 22

HIDDEN STRENGTH: MOTIONLESS DEFENSE (FREEZE, FEIGNED DEATH, SUBMISSION)

Sometimes, when we are very scared our bodies become frozen. In the animal world, opossums are famous for feigning death: when they appear dead, they are less desirable to a predator. Deer are famous for standing still in the woods, allowing themselves to blend into the scenery and become less visible to the roving eye of a predator. Bomji responded to threat by freezing, so the coyote didn't notice him.

page 10

page 17

HIDDEN STRENGTH: SEEKING CLOSENESS FOR PROTECTION AND COMFORT FROM SAFE PEOPLE

When a child faces scary things, danger, or overwhelming stress, the child will feel the need to be close to a protective adult, just like Spotty and Bomji reached out to Teacher Owl.

page 23

page 31

HIDDEN STRENGTH: ORIENTING RESPONSE

When animals first sense danger, just like Bomji and Spotty hearing the tree's branch break in the woods, they stop what they are doing and try to locate the source of danger. This is called the orienting response.

When humans sense something new or unusual in our environment, we move our eyes and turn our heads or bodies to observe our surroundings. Orienting helps us to spot what's dangerous as well as what's safe and beautiful in our environment. This is how we gather information from our environment.

In this story, Teacher Owl employed the orienting response to help Bomji. Teacher Owl directed him to notice positive and safe things in his current environment. Bomji not only noticed the bee and blue sky, he also noticed flowers growing in the school playground.

page 8

page 29

Anne Westcott's life work focuses on helping people (young and old) who have been having a hard time to understand how their bodies give them hidden strengths. She is a clinical social worker and psychotherapist who lives in Concord, Massachusetts with her husband and two daughters, and she loves to be outside and moving, no matter what the weather.

Growing up with manga (comics) in Taiwan, **C. C. Alicia Hu** knows the secret of learning new things is to look at words and pictures together. That's why she enjoys making stories like this series! As a practicing psychologist in Moscow, Idaho and Pullman, Washington, she also enjoys using simple body exercises to help people feel better about themselves.

HOW LITTLE COYOTE FOUND HIS SECRET STRENGTH

A Story About How to Get Through Hard Times

In a deep dark forest, Little Coyote grows up with tough gang of big strong coyotes. They are cruel, call him names, and order him about all day long.

Little Coyote is too small to run away or to stand up for himself, so he learns to do what he's told and makes his body small so nobody notices him. Then, one day he goes on an adventure and ends up discovering new hidden strengths that he never knew he had.

This therapeutic picture book is written to help children aged 4–10 and adults to talk about difficult experiences growing up (including things they may still be going through), and explores how they can affect how your body feels and reacts to things. It is followed by easy to read advice for adults on how to help your child.

HOW SPRINKLE THE PIG ESCAPED THE RIVER OF TEARS
**A Story About Being Apart
from Loved Ones**

Sprinkle the Pig has moved to a new house with a new family, but he misses his old family. On his first day at school his classmate yells at him, and everything gets too much. He cries and cries, and soon the tears become a river and carry him away! Wise monkey spots Sprinkle, but he is too far away. Can he help Sprinkle to find hidden strengths to survive the river of tears?

This therapeutic picture book is written to help children aged 4–10 and adults to talk about being separated from or losing loved ones, and explores how difficult experiences can affect how your body feels and reacts to things. It is followed by easy to read advice for adults on how to help your child.